W9-CGY-785

Super Simple ORIGAMI

32 NEW DESIGNS

John Montroll

Dover Publications, Inc., Mineola, New York

To Josh and Mel

Bibliographical Note

Super Simple Origami: 32 New Designs is a new work, first published by Dover Publications, Inc., in 2011.

International Standard Book Number
ISBN-13: 978-0-486-48361-0
ISBN-10: 0-486-48361-4

Manufactured in the United States by LSC Communications
48361402   2017
www.doverpublications.com

Introduction

Origami is so much fun. Here is a collection of 32 simple models. Most of these are original designs, while a few are variations of traditional models. Many themes are covered, including boats, fish, insects, birds, reptiles, chess pieces, and more. It is my hope that you will enjoy origami and aspire to learn more.

In this colorful collection, a photo of each model is shown. All the models are simple and most are very simple. The number of steps is a good indication of the level of simplicity. If you are new to origami, I recommend that you start with the first projects.

The illustrations conform to the internationally accepted Randlett-Yoshizawa conventions. Origami paper is colored on one side and white on the other. The colored side is represented by the shadings in the diagrams. Origami supplies can be found in arts and craft shops, or visit Dover Publications online at www.doverpublications.com, or OrigamiUSA at www.origami-usa.org or Amazon at www.amazon.com.

Happy folding,

John Montroll
http://www.johnmontroll.com

Contents

Symbols   Page 6

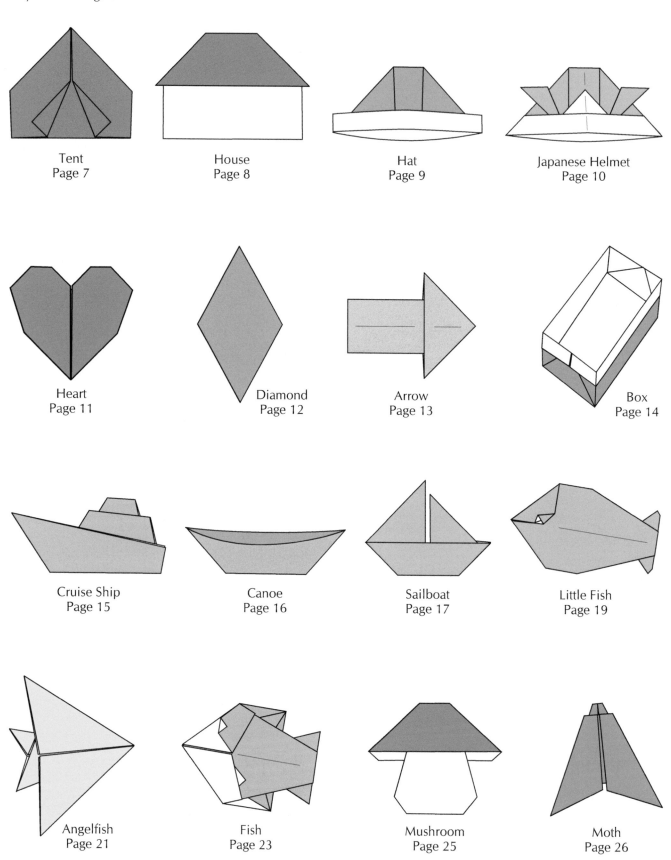

Tent
Page 7

House
Page 8

Hat
Page 9

Japanese Helmet
Page 10

Heart
Page 11

Diamond
Page 12

Arrow
Page 13

Box
Page 14

Cruise Ship
Page 15

Canoe
Page 16

Sailboat
Page 17

Little Fish
Page 19

Angelfish
Page 21

Fish
Page 23

Mushroom
Page 25

Moth
Page 26

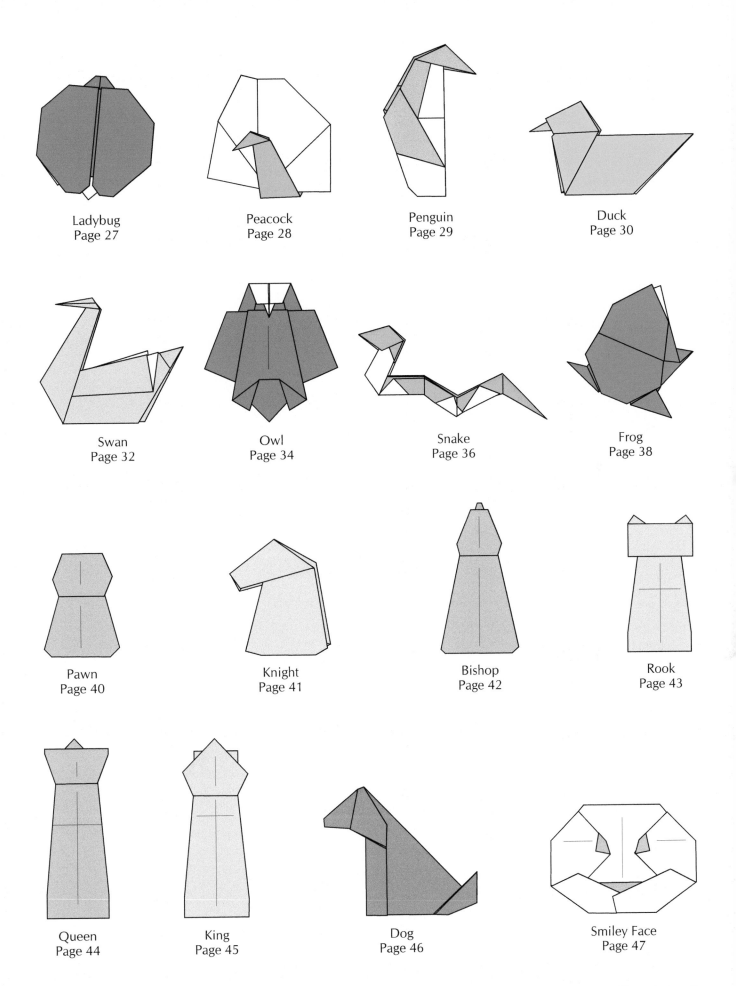

Ladybug
Page 27

Peacock
Page 28

Penguin
Page 29

Duck
Page 30

Swan
Page 32

Owl
Page 34

Snake
Page 36

Frog
Page 38

Pawn
Page 40

Knight
Page 41

Bishop
Page 42

Rook
Page 43

Queen
Page 44

King
Page 45

Dog
Page 46

Smiley Face
Page 47

Symbols

Lines

— — — — — — — —   Valley fold, fold in front.

— · — · · — · — · — ·   Mountain fold, fold behind.

———————   Crease line.

· · · · · · · · · · · · · · · · ·   X-ray or guide line.

Arrows

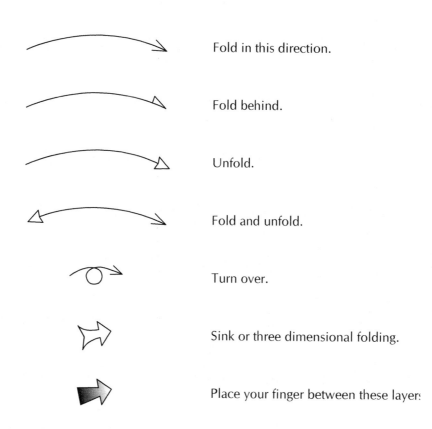

Fold in this direction.

Fold behind.

Unfold.

Fold and unfold.

Turn over.

Sink or three dimensional folding.

Place your finger between these layer:

Tent

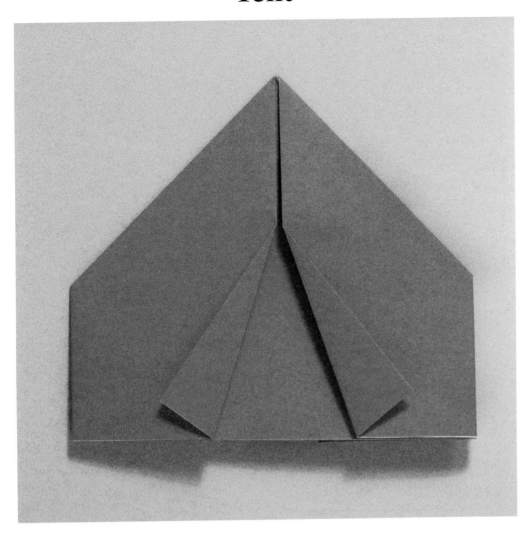

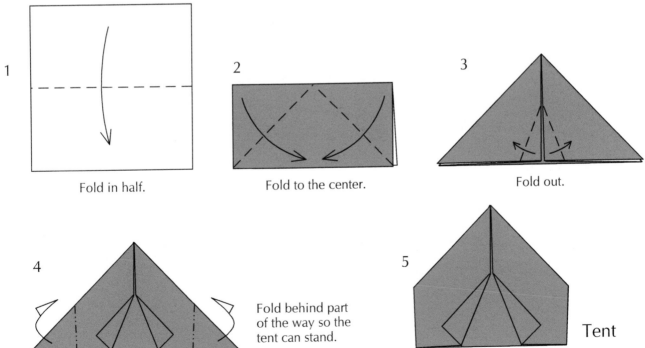

1   Fold in half.

2   Fold to the center.

3   Fold out.

4   Fold behind part of the way so the tent can stand.

5   Tent

House

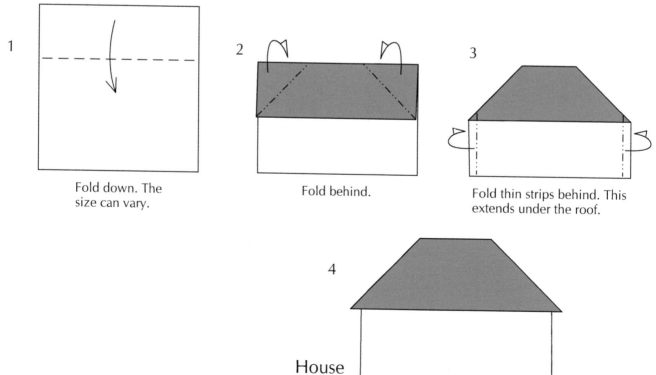

1 Fold down. The size can vary.

2 Fold behind.

3 Fold thin strips behind. This extends under the roof.

4

House

Hat

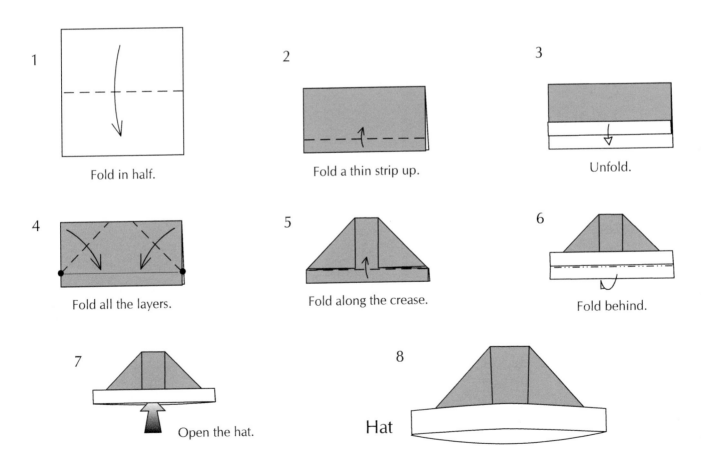

1

Fold in half.

2

Fold a thin strip up.

3

Unfold.

4

Fold all the layers.

5

Fold along the crease.

6

Fold behind.

7

Open the hat.

8

Hat

Japanese Helmet

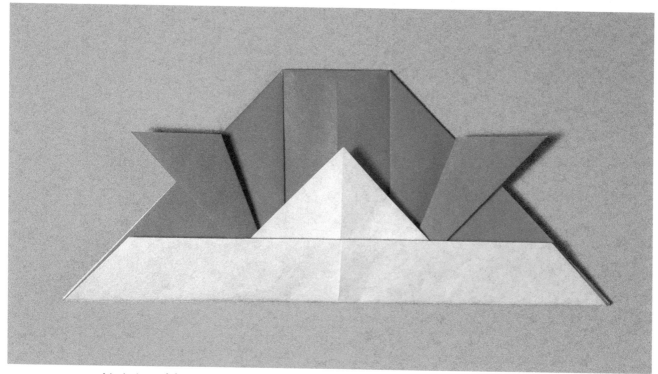

Variation of the Traditional Samurai Hat

1

Fold and unfold.

2

Fold in half.

3

Fold both layers near the

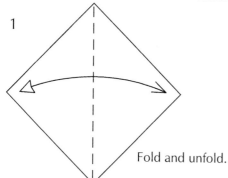

4

Fold up.

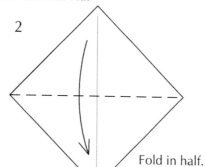

5

Fold the corners out.

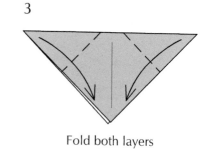

6

Fold the top layer up and repeat behind.

7

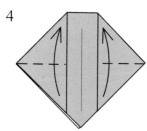

Fold the top layer up and repeat behind.

8

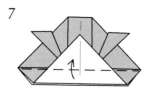

Open.

9

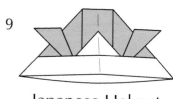

Japanese Helmet

Heart

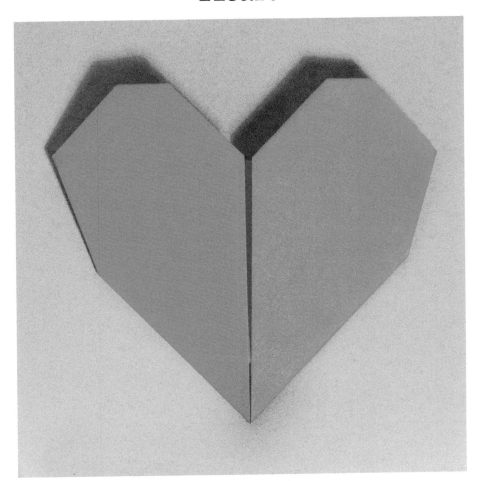

1

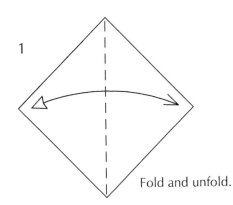

Fold and unfold.

2

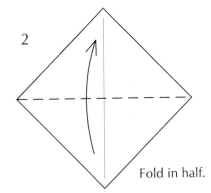

Fold in half.

3

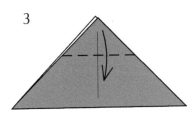

Fold both layers
near the

4

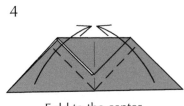

Fold to the center.

5

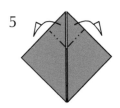

Fold behind.

6

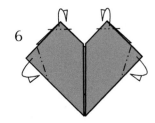

Fold all the layers behind.

7

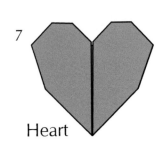

Heart

Diamond

1

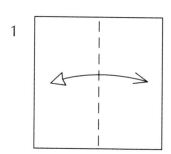

Fold and unfold.

2

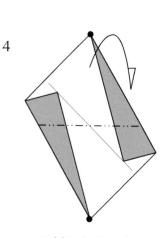

Bring the corner
to the crease.

3

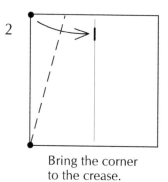

Bring the corner to
the crease. Rotate.

4

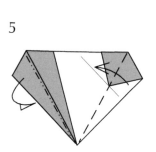

Fold in half so the
dots will meet.

5

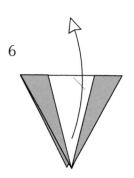

Fold in front and behind.

6

Unfold the top flap.

7

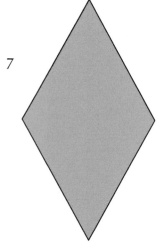

Diamond

Arrow

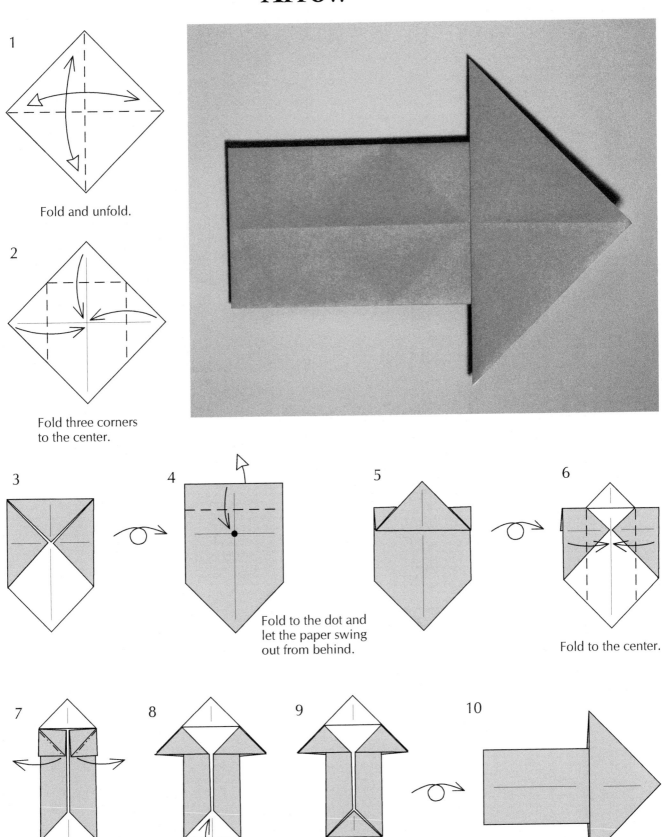

1

Fold and unfold.

2

Fold three corners to the center.

3

4

Fold to the dot and let the paper swing out from behind.

5

6

Fold to the center.

7

Pull out the top layers.

8

Fold up.

9

Turn over and rotate.

10

Arrow

Box

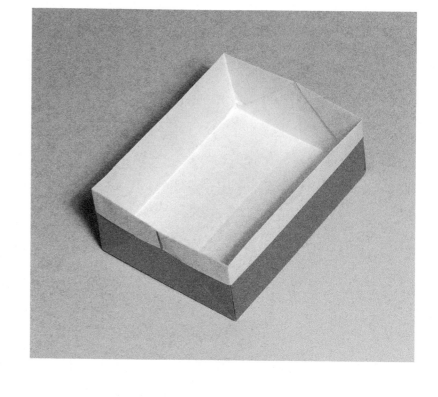

1
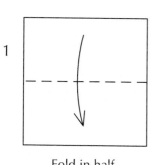
Fold in half.

2
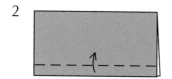
Fold a thin strip up.
Repeat behind.

3
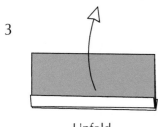
Unfold.

4
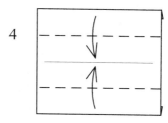
Fold to the center.

5
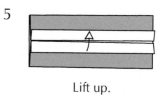
Lift up.

6

Fold to the crease.

7

Fold one layer
along the crease.

8
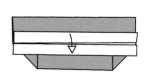
Repeat steps 5–7
on the top.

9
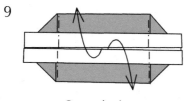
Open the box.

10
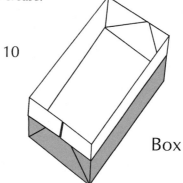
Box

Cruise Ship

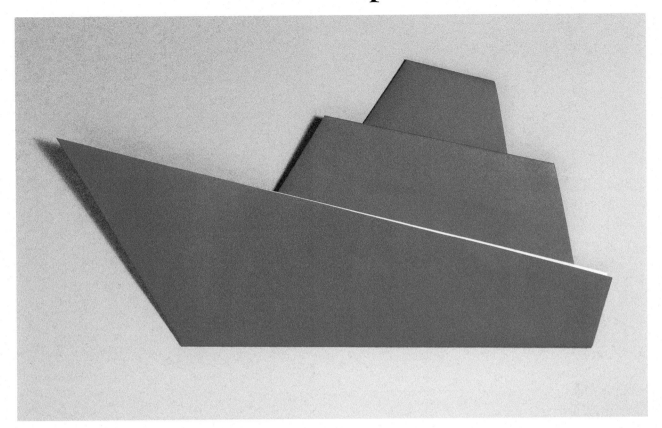

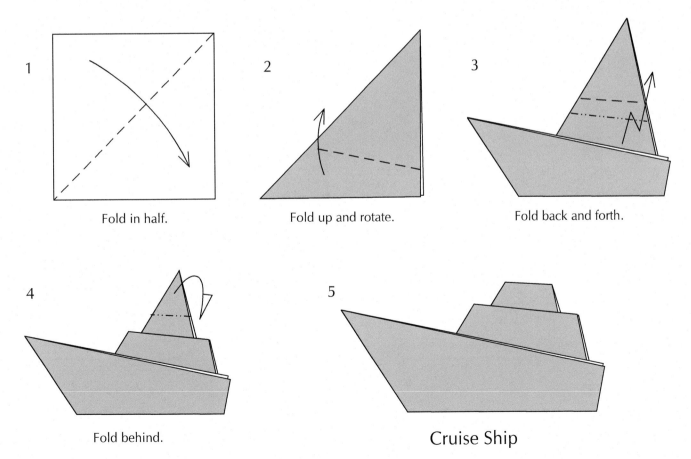

1

Fold in half.

2

Fold up and rotate.

3

Fold back and forth.

4

Fold behind.

5

Cruise Ship

Canoe

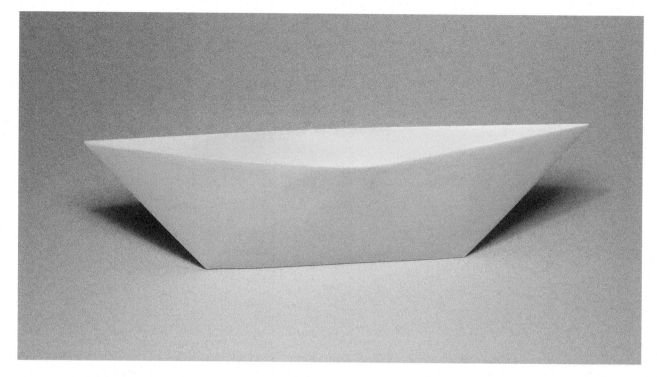

1

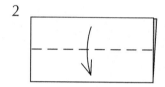

Fold in half.

2

Fold the top
layer in half.

3

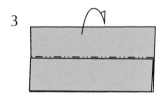

Fold in half behind.

4

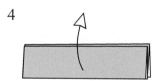

Unfold and repeat behind.

5

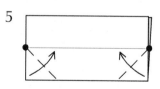

Fold all the layers.

6

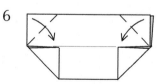

Fold the top layer to the
front and repeat behind.

7

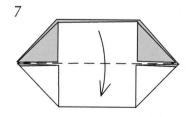

Fold the top layer
and repeat behind.

8

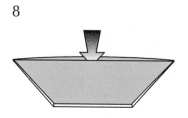

Open the canoe.

9

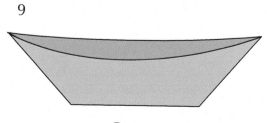

Canoe

Sailboat

Variation on the Traditional Sailboat

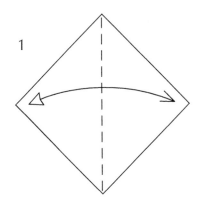

1

Fold and unfold.

2

Fold in half.

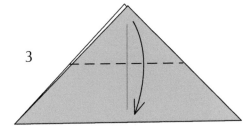

3

Fold both layers to the bottom.

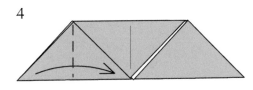

4

Fold to the right.

5

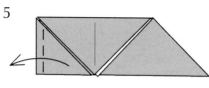

Fold to the left.

6

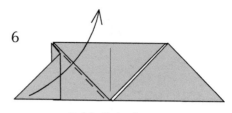

Fold all the layers.

7

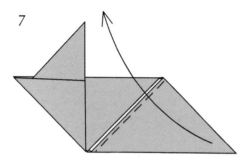

Fold the layers up.

8

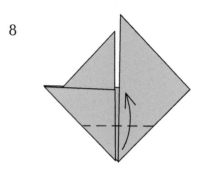

Fold the layers up.

9

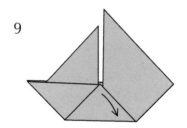

Fold the triangle down
so it becomes the stand
for the sailboat.

10

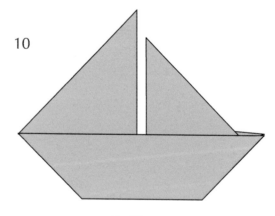

Sailboat

Little Fish

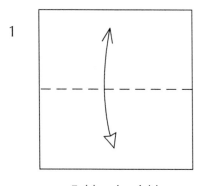

1 Fold and unfold.

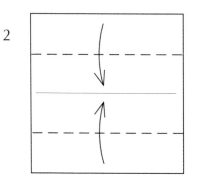

2 Fold to the center.

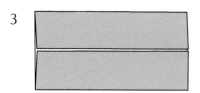

3

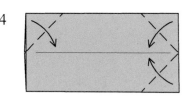

4 Fold three corners towards the center.

5

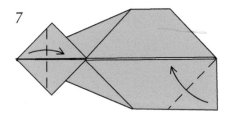

6

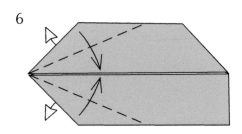

Fold to the center and let the
paper swing out from behind.

7

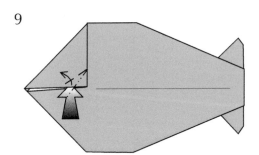

Make two folds.

8

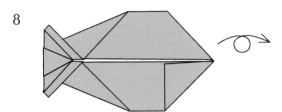

9

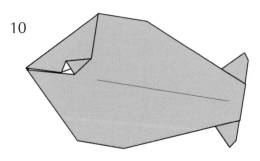

Place your finger
between the layers and
spread a little to make

10

Little Fish

Angelfish

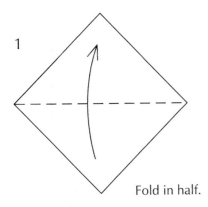

1

Fold in half.

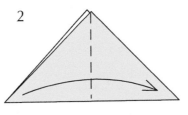

2

Fold in half.

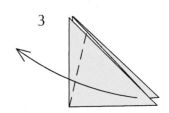

3

Fold the top flap.

4

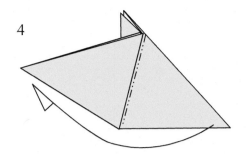

Fold behind.

5

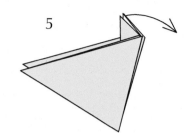

Pull out the inside flap.

6

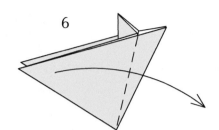

Fold the top flap along
the crease. Rotate.

7

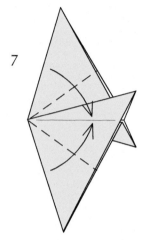

Fold to the center.

8

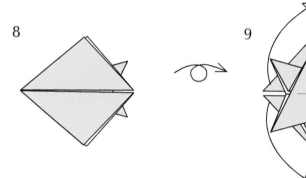

9

Fold to the center and let the
paper swing out from behind.

10

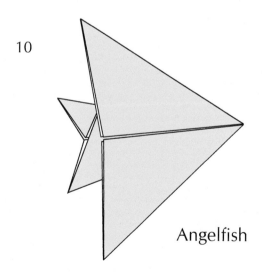

Angelfish

Fish

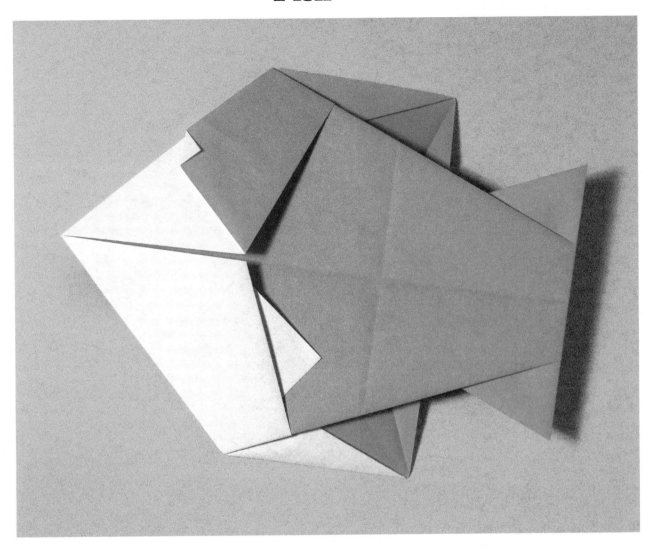

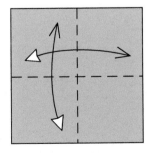

1

Fold and unfold.

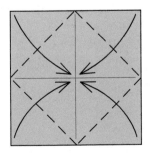

2

Fold the corners
to the center.

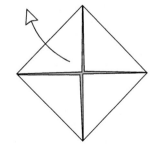

3

Unfold on one side.

4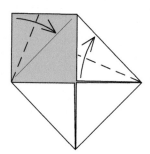

5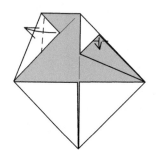

6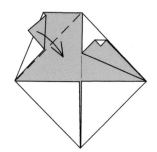

Fold along the crease.

7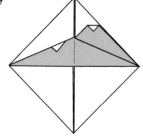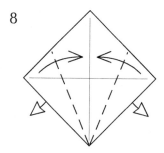

8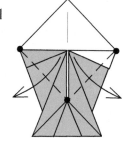

Fold to the center and let the
paper swing out from behind.

9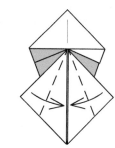

Fold to the center.

10

Fold up.

11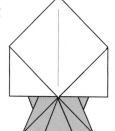

Fold the top layers out.

12

Rotate.

13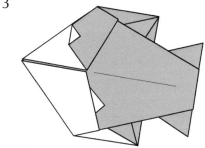

Fish

Mushroom

1

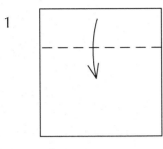

The size can vary.
Every mushroom will
be a bit different.

2

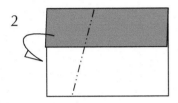

The exact location
of this fold is not
important.

3

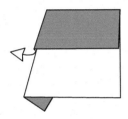

Pull out some paper.

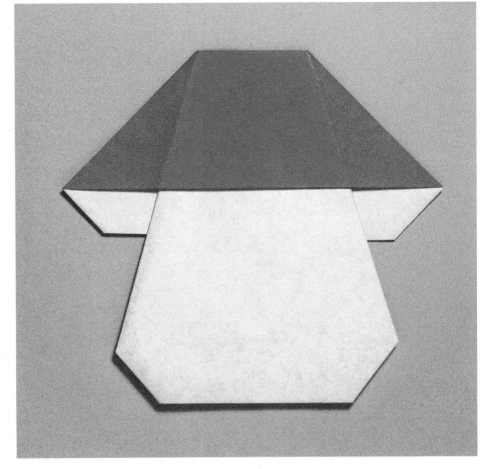

4

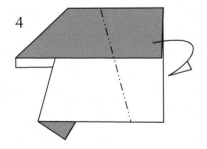

Repeat steps 2–3
on the right.

5

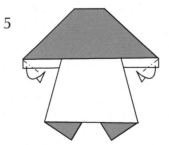

Fold behind.

6

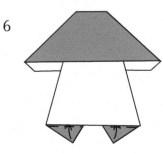

Tuck inside.

7

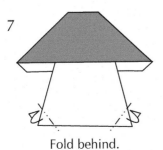

Fold behind.

8

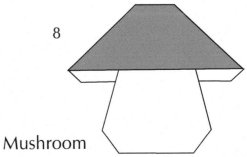

Mushroom

Moth

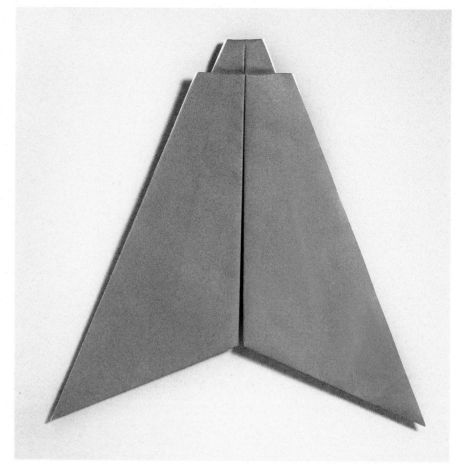

1

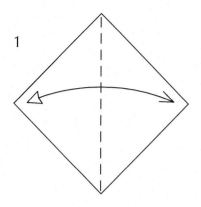

Fold and unfold.

2

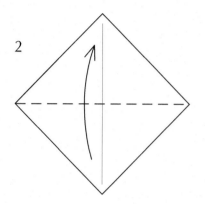

Fold in half.

3

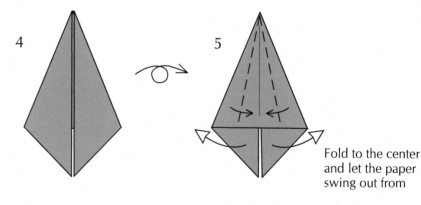

Fold to the center.

4

5

Fold to the center
and let the paper
swing out from

6

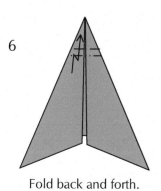

Fold back and forth.

7

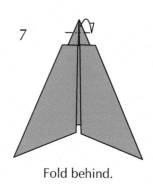

Fold behind.

8

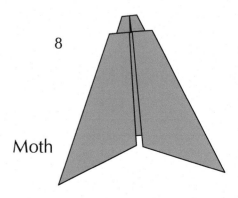

Moth

Ladybug

1

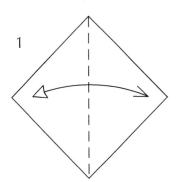

Fold and unfold.

2

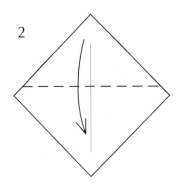

The exact location
is not important.

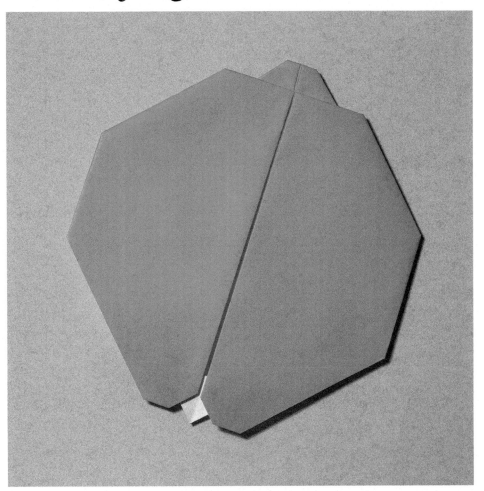

3

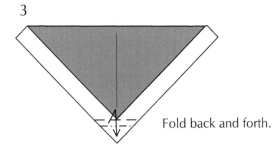

Fold back and forth.

4

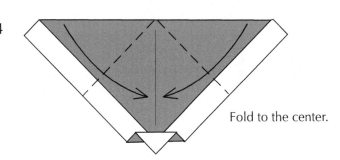

Fold to the center.

5

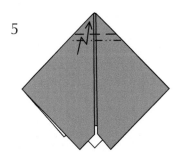

Fold back and forth.

6

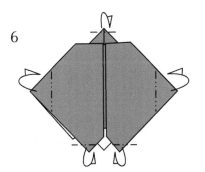

Fold behind at the
head and wings.

7

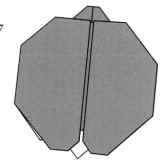

Ladybug

Peacock

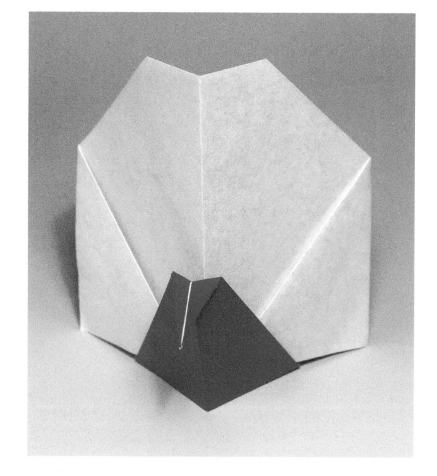

1

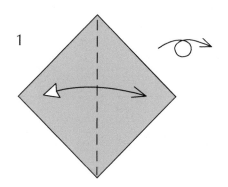

Fold and unfold.

2

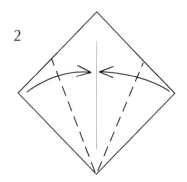

Fold to the center.

3

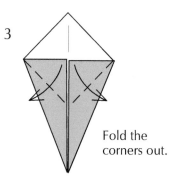

Fold the corners out.

4

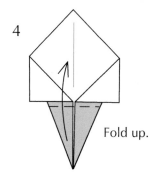

Fold up.

5

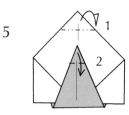

1. Fold behind.
2. Fold the head down.

6

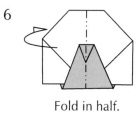

Fold in half.

7

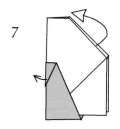

Slide the head up and open the model to spread the plumes.

8

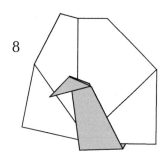

Peacock

Penguin

1

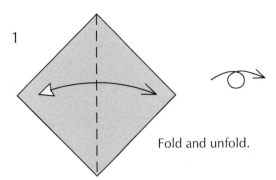

Fold and unfold.

2

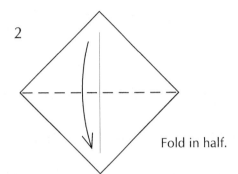

Fold in half.

3

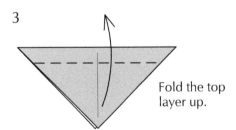

Fold the top layer up.

4

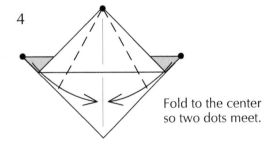

Fold to the center so two dots meet.

5

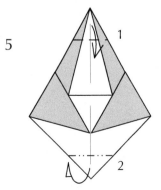

1. Fold down.
2. Fold behind.

6

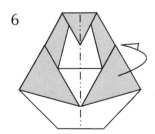

Fold in half.

7

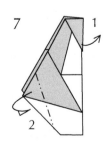

1. Slide the head.
2. Fold inside and repeat behind.

8

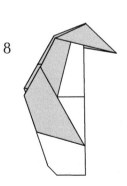

Penguin

Duck

1

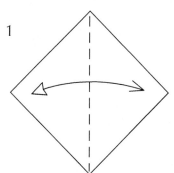

Fold and unfold.

2

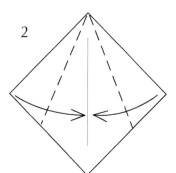

Fold to the center.

3

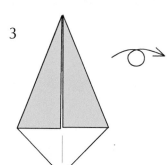

4

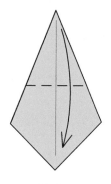

Fold down.

5

Fold up.

6

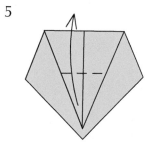

Fold back and forth.

7

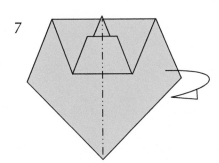

Fold behind and rotate.

8

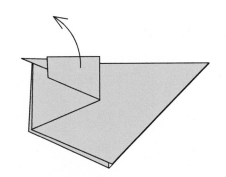

Lift up the neck
and head.

9

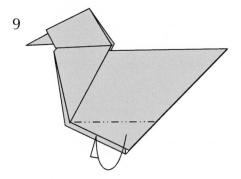

Fold inside and
repeat behind.

10

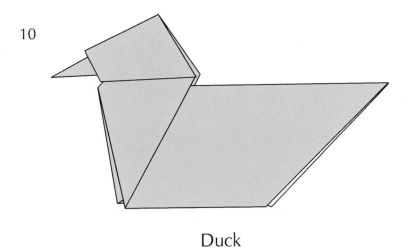

Duck

Swan

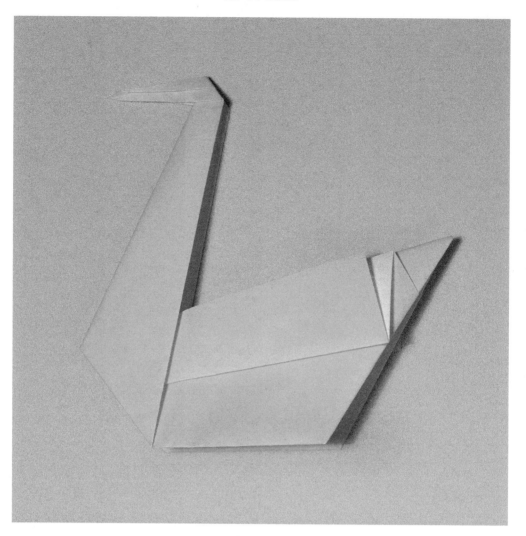

1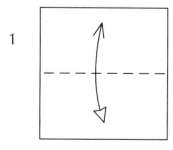

Fold and unfold.

2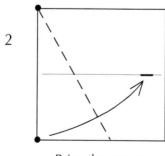

Bring the corner
to the crease.

3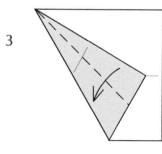

Rotate.

4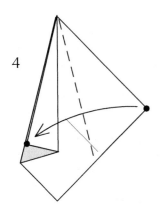

The dots will meet.

5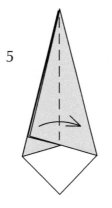

Fold the top layer.

6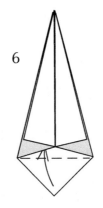

Tuck inside.

7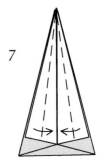

Fold to the center.

8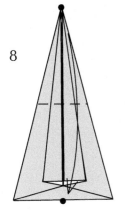

Fold down.

9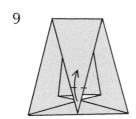

Fold up.

10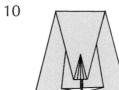

11

Fold to the center.

12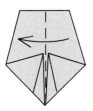

Fold in half
and rotate.

13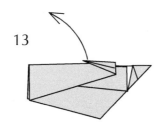

Slide the neck and head.

14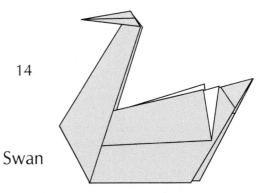

Swan

Owl

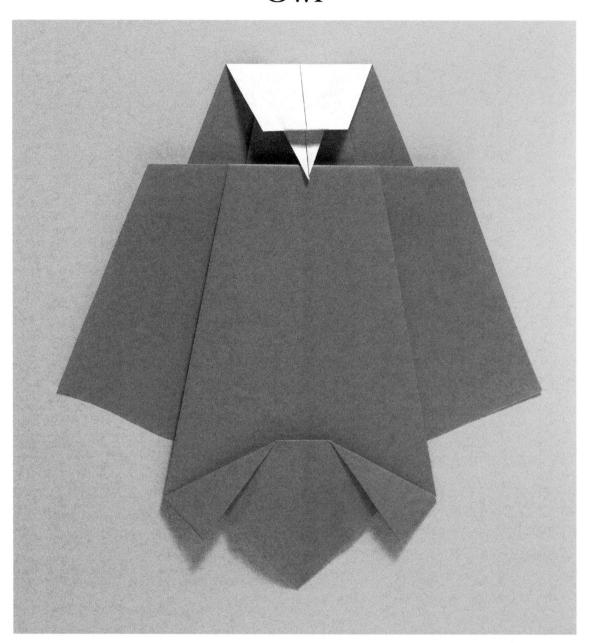

1

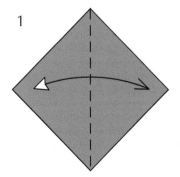

Fold and unfold.

2

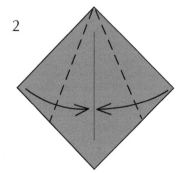

Fold to the center.

3

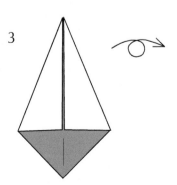

4

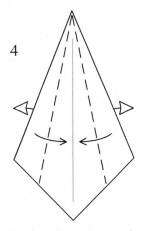

Fold to the center and
let the paper swing out
from behind.

5

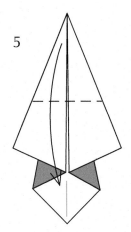

Fold down.

6

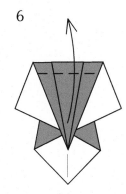

Fold up.

7

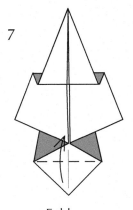

Fold up.

8

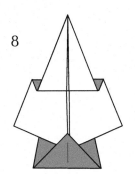

9

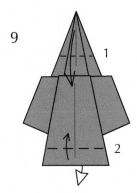

1. Fold down.
2. Fold up and let the paper
swing out from behind.

10

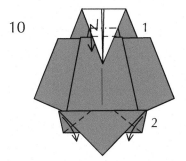

1. Fold back and forth.
2. Fold down.

11

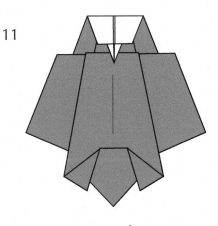

Owl

Snake

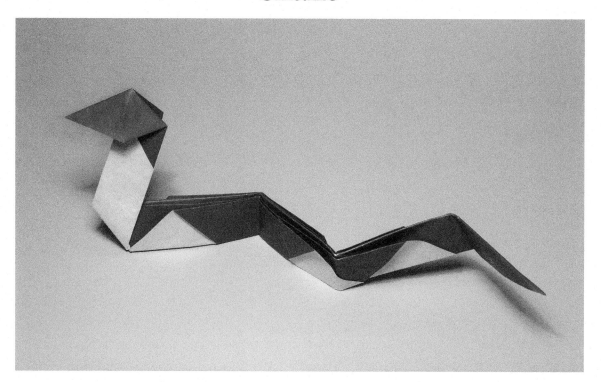

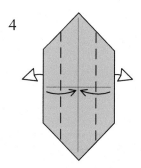

1

Fold and unfold.

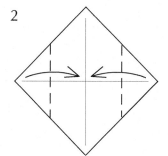

2

Fold two corners
to the center.

3

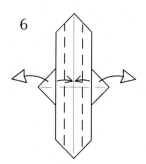

4

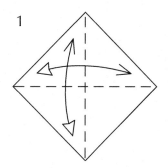

Fold to the center and let the
paper swing out from behind.

5

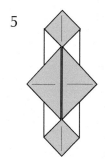

6

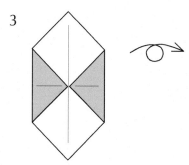

Fold to the center and let the
paper swing out from behind.

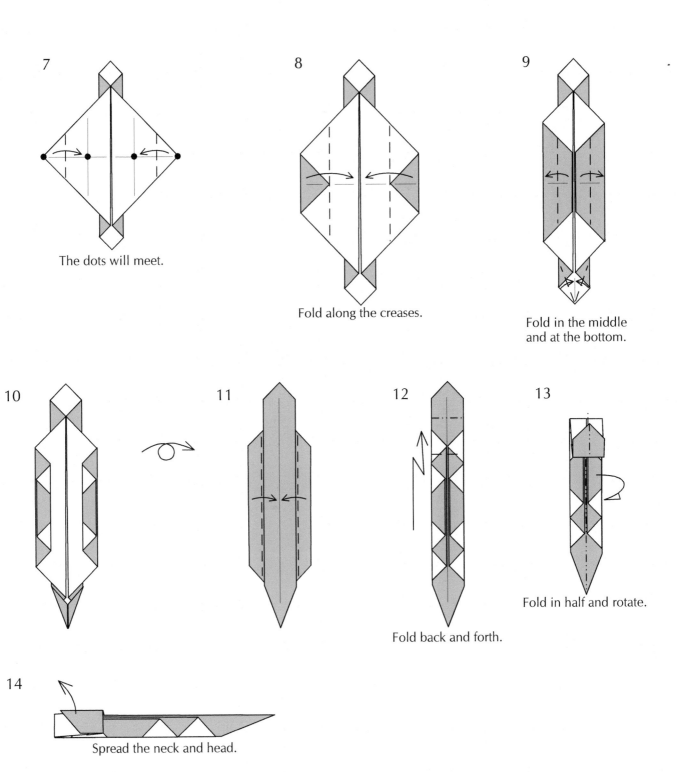

7

The dots will meet.

8

Fold along the creases.

9

Fold in the middle
and at the bottom.

10

11

12

Fold back and forth.

13

Fold in half and rotate.

14

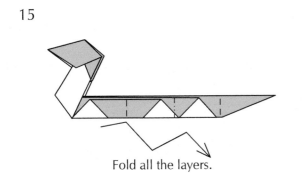

Spread the neck and head.

15

Fold all the layers.

16

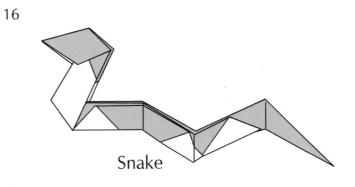

Snake

Frog

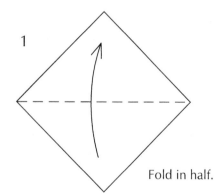

1

Fold in half.

2

Fold a thin strip.

3

Fold to the center.

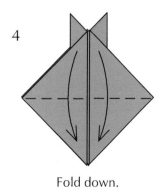

4

Fold down.

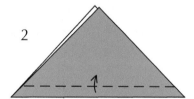

5

Spread the paper.

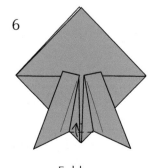

6

Fold up.

7

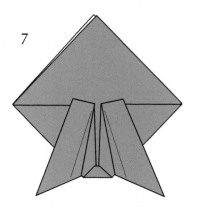

8

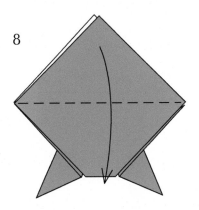

Fold both layers down.

9

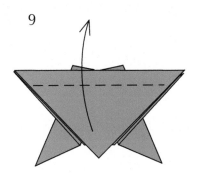

Fold both layers up.

10

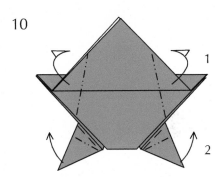

1. Fold the front legs straight down so the frog can sit.
2. Bend the hind legs.

11

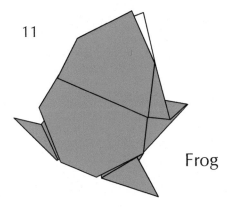

Frog

Pawn

1

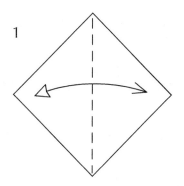

Fold and unfold.

2

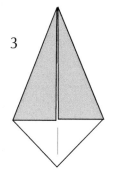

Fold to the center.

3

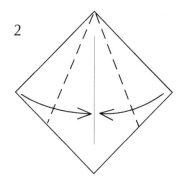

4

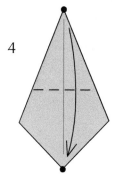

Fold down.

5

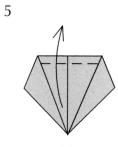

Fold up.

6

 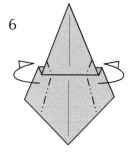

Fold behind.

7

 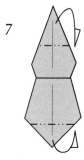

Fold behind.

8

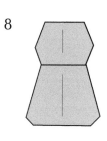

Pawn

Knight

1

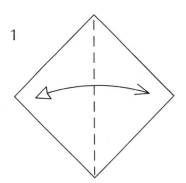

Fold and unfold.

2

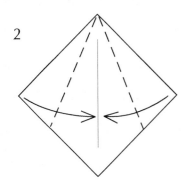

Fold to the center.

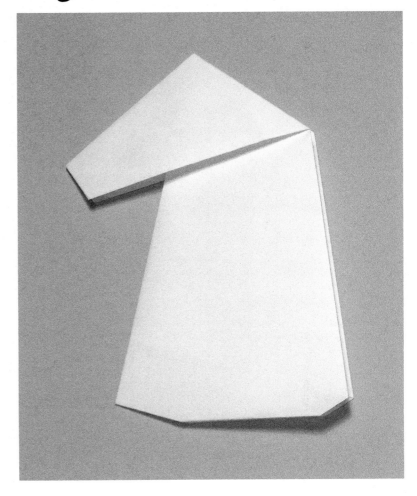

3

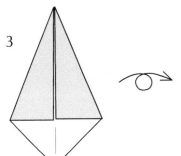

4

Fold down to the dot. The
dotted lines show the x-ray
view from behind.

5

Fold behind.

6

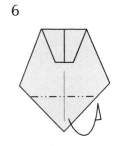

Fold behind.

7

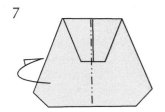

Fold in half.

8

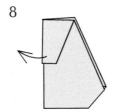

Slide the head.

9

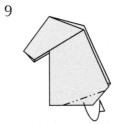

Fold inside and
repeat behind.

10

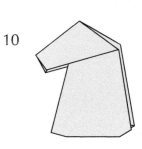

Knight

Bishop

1
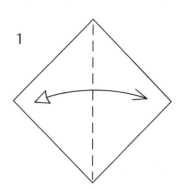
Fold and unfold.

2
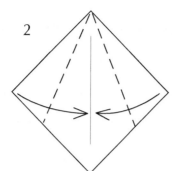
Fold to the center.

3
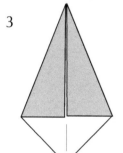

4
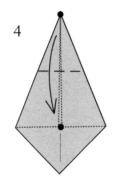
Fold down to the dot. The dotted lines show the x-ray view from behind.

5
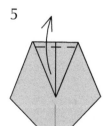
Fold up.

6
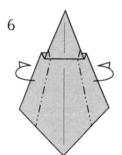
Fold behind.

7

Fold back and forth.

8
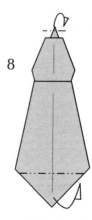
Fold behind.

9
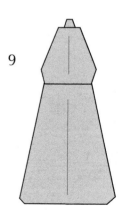
Bishop

Rook

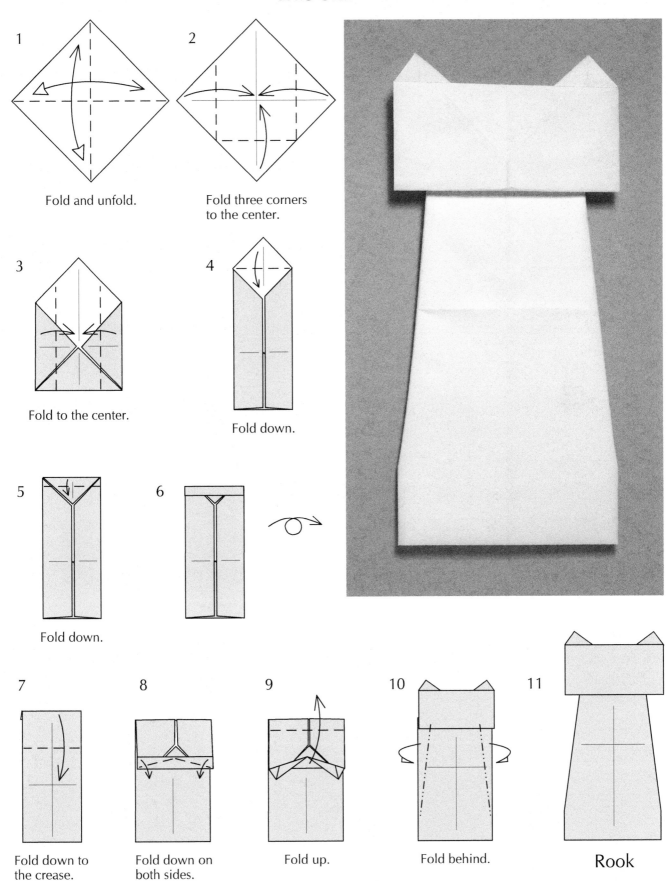

1 Fold and unfold.

2 Fold three corners to the center.

3 Fold to the center.

4 Fold down.

5 Fold down.

6

7 Fold down to the crease.

8 Fold down on both sides.

9 Fold up.

10 Fold behind.

11 Rook

Queen

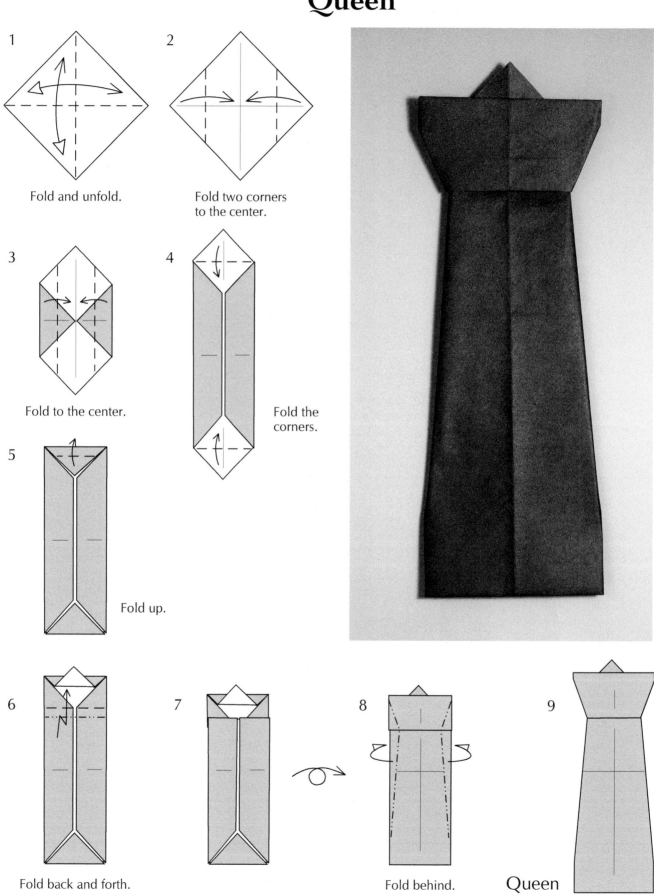

1

Fold and unfold.

2

Fold two corners to the center.

3

Fold to the center.

4

Fold the corners.

5

Fold up.

6

Fold back and forth.

7

8

Fold behind.

9

Queen

King

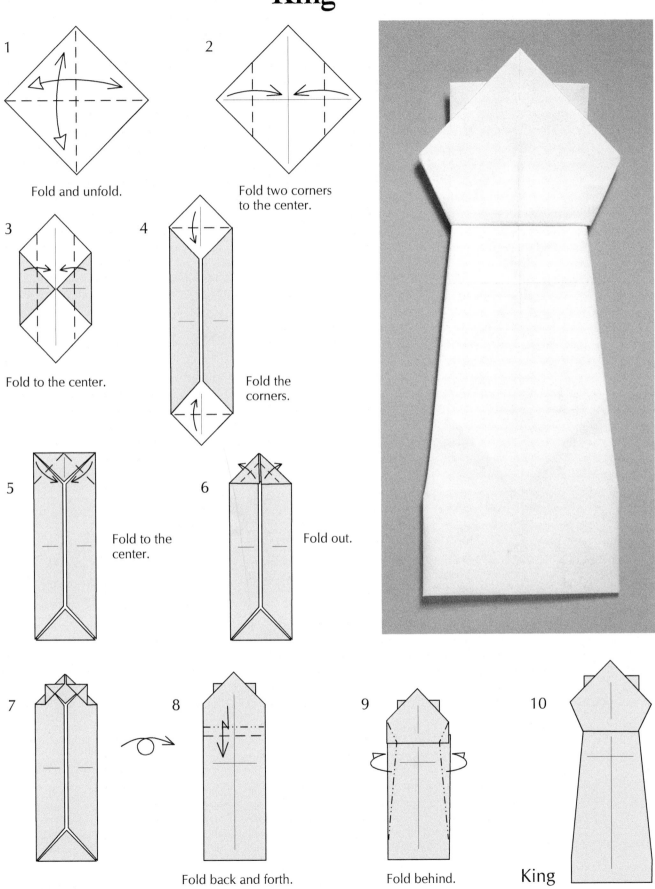

1 Fold and unfold.

2 Fold two corners to the center.

3 Fold to the center.

4 Fold the corners.

5 Fold to the center.

6 Fold out.

7

8 Fold back and forth.

9 Fold behind.

10 King

Dog

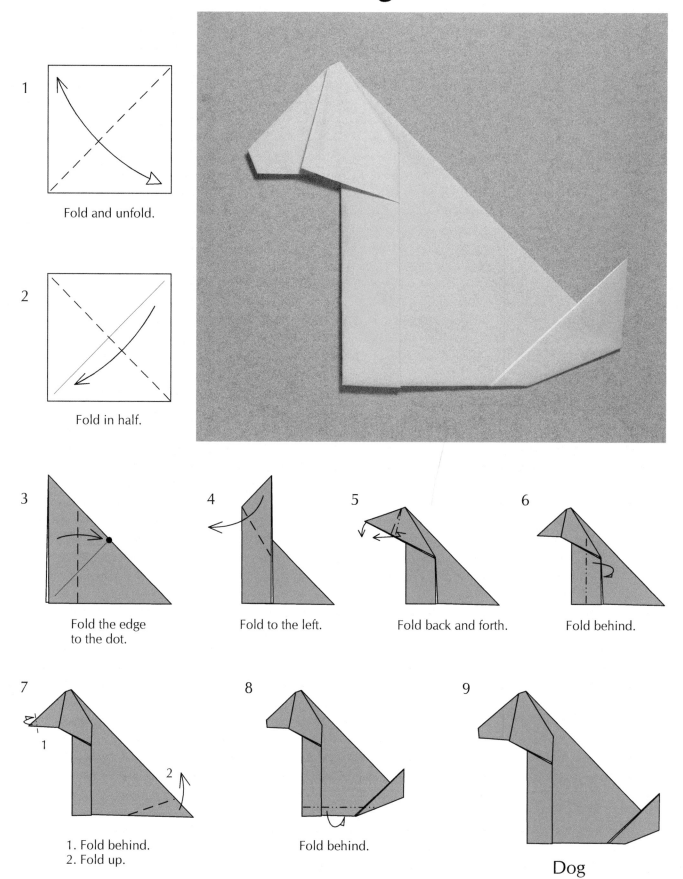

1

Fold and unfold.

2

Fold in half.

3

Fold the edge
to the dot.

4

Fold to the left.

5

Fold back and forth.

6

Fold behind.

7

1. Fold behind.
2. Fold up.

8

Fold behind.

9

Dog

Smiley Face

1

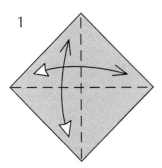

Fold and unfold.

2

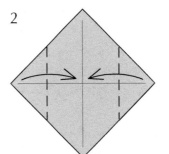

Fold two corners
to the center.

3

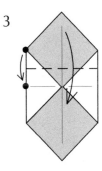

Fold down so
the dots meet.

4

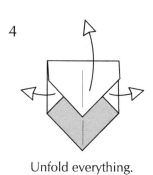

Unfold everything.

5

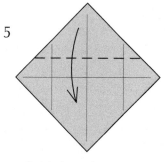

Fold along the crease.

6

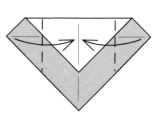

Fold along the creases.

7

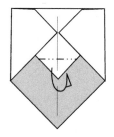

Fold behind.

8

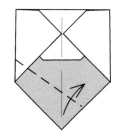

Fold up.

9

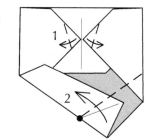

1. Fold the eyes.
2. Fold up.

10

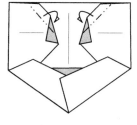

Fold behind
at the eyes.

11

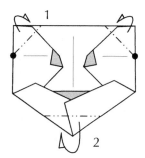

Fold behind in order.

12

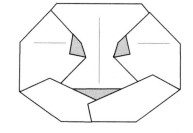

Smiley Face